HEAD VASES
Identification & Values

Kathleen Cole

HEAD VASES
Identification & Values

Kathleen Cole

COLLECTOR BOOKS
A Division of Schroeder Publishing Co., Inc.

Additional copies of this book may be ordered from:

COLLECTOR BOOKS
P.O. Box 3009
Paducah, Kentucky 42002-3009

@14.95. Add $2.00 for postage and handling.

Dedication

This book is dedicated to my beloved husband Jack who died of cancer on June 29, 1984.

Acknowledgments

My thanks to my daughter Melanie who has helped me "get it all together." To my doctor and friend, John McCarter, who so patiently helped me with the photographs. To Dr. Tom Elkin, Michael Thienes, Mike Himes, Ralph Burt, Bette White, Robert Persons, Bonnie Herron, Beverly and Oleta Brumfields, Jim and Carol Tharp dealers and friends too numerous to mention. To my long time friend, Jane Basden, for the proofing and typing. Thanks to all of those whose support and encouragement helped me to do the book. Most of all, I thank "My Heavenly Father," for without His help this book would never have been published.

Foreword

Collecting antiques has been a hobby of mine for more than 30 years. In fact, I have been a lover of "old things" since my childhood. One of my greatest thrills as a young girl was to visit our relatives who lived in the country. I remember the old kitchen clock, the crockery milk pitchers, the pressed glass cake stand, and many other things too numerous to mention.

My earliest recollection of collecting was figurines; most of them were Occupied Japan.

My first real collection as an adult was a pressed glass pattern, "Horsemint." My first piece was a preserve stand given to me by my grandmother.

Later on, through the advice of an antique dealer I began to collect Nippon china. I continued to collect it until the prices advanced so much that it moved out of my price range. Because of the continuing price rise, I lost most of my enthusiasm for collecting.

One day a customer, Mrs Dorothy Biggs, came into the stamp and coin shop where I worked. One subject led to another, and she told me she was collecting "head vases." To my knowledge I had never seen one. She showed me pictures of them, and I thought they were beautiful.

The next time I went to the flea market I began to see them. Every time I saw one I'd wonder if Mrs. Biggs had it. I became so fascinated that my old desire to collect came back. At first, children were my specialty, but it was not long before I realized it was too limited. My interest grew, and the exciting search for heads began.

The original purpose for these, I'm told, was for florists' arrangements. Since most of them were small, it was difficult to put enough flowers in them to be profitable; so they became "dust catchers" on the back room shelves in florists' shops.

My search began in these back rooms where I found many different ones at very reasonable prices.

Most of these vases were sold to florists through pottery importers since a great many of them were made in Japan. The only importer I was able to contact was National Pottery Company. They told me since these vases were more than ten years old they had no catalogs on them. Many of them have names, numbers, and dates on the bottom. Hundreds have no names, nor numbers, or only "made in Japan."

This book will by no means picture them all. I have more than 1,000, and I have seen perhaps hundreds in other collections that I do not have.

The current values in this book should be merely a guide. The condition will have a great bearing on the values, as well as rarity and availability.

As nearly as possible, these heads will be pictured in groups—ladies, (young) ladies, teenagers, famous people, oriental, religious, clowns, animals, art deco, men, children, babies, wall pockets, and miscellaneous. Included will be some that perhaps were not made for flowers, but they are head vases nevertheless.

Each head will be identified by company, number and date (if any), size and price.

No doubt there will be discrepancies, and I apologize for that.

Having collected "Head Vases" for more than ten years, I have learned a lot and thought I might pass along some of the information to you.

1. Where to find: Most of my heads came from the back rooms of old florist shops, flea markets, garage sales, antique malls, and from friends. Be sure and make your friends aware of your collection. Even if they don't have any, they may have an acquaintance who does.

2. What to buy: Be sure to buy only the ones that you like, can afford, and that are in good condition. Remember, if the time comes that you want to sell them, only those in good condition will sell. Do not be tempted to buy any that you don't like just because you do not have them.

3. What to pay: Prices vary so much from dealer to dealer, different sections of the country, and even at garage and carport sales. Please do not set a price limit. If you do, you will be a frustrated collector. Don't hesitate to walk away from a head you like if the price is too high for you. On the other hand, if it is unique and high, buy it anyway. I would rather have one that is special than two or three common ones.

4. What to do with duplicates: Find someone who also collects and do some trading with them. Also, you will find many dealers who are willing to trade. Even if you have to pay a difference, it is better than having two alike.

5. Keep records: Many of the heads have company names and numbers. You will find this to be very helpful in knowing which ones you have. Set up a small notebook with sections for each company and their numbers. Unfortunately hundreds of them have no marks or numbers and it is here that we have trouble. In this case, we must depend upon our memory and that doesn't always work well. If it looks familiar, and you have a question in your mind, don't buy it until you check.

I hope these hints and the book will be helpful to you. Happy Head Hunting!

Contents

Ladies

PLATE 1

INARCO
#E190 E/L
8½″ Tall
(1961)

PLATE 2

INARCO
#E190/L
7″ Tall
(1961)

INARCO
#E190/M
5″ Tall
(1961)

INARCO
#E190/S
4¾″ Tall
(1961)

PLATE 3

NAPCO
#C4891A
(1961)
8½″ Tall

PLATE 4	RUBENS #497/M 6½″ Tall	No Mark 7″ Tall	INARCO #E2104 7″ Tall	INARCO #E2104 7″ Tall

PLATE 5   INARCO
#E 2966
11″ Tall

PLATE 6   NAPCOWARE
#C 7498
11″ Tall

PLATE 7   NAPCO
#659/MA
(1959)
5″ Tall

NAPCOWARE
#C569
5″ Tall

NAPCOWARE
#C348
7″ Tall

PLATE 8   No Mark   No Mark   No Mark   No Mark
                #S673B   #S673A   #S348B   #C348A
                4¼″ Tall   4¼″ Tall   6½″ Tall   6½″ Tall
                (no glove)   (glove)   (no glove)   (glove)

 PLATE 9

RELPO   RELPO   RELPO
#A-1373S   #A1197   A-1229
4½″ Tall   5″ Tall   6½″ Tall

PLATE 10

JAPAN   No Mark   JAPAN
5″ Tall   5″ Tall   5″ Tall

PLATE 11   No Mark   No Mark   No Mark
                  6″ Tall   6″ Tall   5″ Tall

PLATE 12   VCAGCO   LEFTON'S   No Mark
                  5¼″ Tall   #2705   #2359
                                   6½″ Tall   6½″ Tall

| PLATE 13 | INARCO
#E969/S
4½″ Tall | NAPCO
#C3342C
4½″ Tall | RUBEN
#498X
5″ Tall | RUBENS
#499B
6″ Tall |

| PLATE 14 | No Mark
#C6018
5½″ Tall | INARCO
#E-191/M/c
5½″ Tall | ROBENS
ORIGINALS
#500
(1959)
5½″ Tall |

PLATE 15   Inarco   No Mark   Inarco   No Mark
              #E-1066   5″ Tall   #E-969/M   5″ Tall
              (1963)   (1963)
              4½″ Tall   5½″ Tall

PLATE 16   JAPAN   INARCO   NAPCO   NAPCO
              5½″ Tall   #E1065   #C3959A   #C2633A
                         (1963)   (1959)   (1956)
                         5½″ Tall   5½″ Tall   5½″ Tall
                                    (Bristle eye
                                    lashes)

INARCO	INARCO	INARCO	INARCO
#E1755	#E1756	#E1610	#E1062
(Lady Aileen)	(Lady Aileen)	(1964)	6″ Tall
(1964)	(1964)	5″ Tall	
3½″ Tall	5½″ Tall		

PLATE 18	LEFTON'S	INARCO	R/B	RELPO
	#624	#E2782	(Paper Label)	#K1817
	5½″ Tall	6″ Tall	5½″ Tall	5½″ Tall

PLATE 19	No Mark	No Mark	INARCO	ENESCO
	5½" Tall	(Japan)	#E1611	(Paper Label)
		5½" Tall	6¼" Tall	5½" Tall

PLATE 20	RELPO	INARCO	No Mark
	#K1335	#E-241	#5919
	8" Tall	6½" Tall	7½" Tall

16

PLATE 21   PARMA   NAPCOWARE
         #A219   (Paper Label)
         8½″ Tall   #C7474
                8″ Tall

PLATE 22   INARCO   NAPCOWARE
         #E-1069   #6986
         (1963)   9″ Tall
         10″ Tall

PLATE 23　　　　　　　　　　**RUBENS**　　　　　　　　　　No Mark
　　　　　　　　　　　　　　　#530　　　　　　　　　　　　6″ Tall
　　　　　　　　　　　　　　6″ Tall　　　　　　　　　　　(Rare)
　　　　　　　　　　　　　　(Rare)
(Both of these pieces are very unusual. The one on the left is dressed in a horse riding outfit. The one on the right in a marching band outfit.)

PLATE 24　　　Enesco　　　　　No Mark　　　　Lefton's　　　　Lefton's
　　　　　　　(Paper Label)　　　5½″ Tall　　　　#1736　　　　　#2251
　　　　　　　　5″ Tall　　　　　　　　　　　　5½″ Tall　　　　6″ Tall

PLATE 25	No Mark 6″ Tall	THAMES (Paper Label) 6″ Tall	No Mark 6″ Tall	MARY LOU 5½″ Tall

PLATE 26	FLORENCE CERAMICES 7″ Tall	ATLAS (Paper Label) 6″ Tall	RELPO #K1052B 5½″ Tall	No Mark #A602 7″ Tall

| PLATE 27 | **INARCO**
#E402
5½″ Tall | **No Mark**
#A5120
5½″ Tall

**(Probably NAPCO
Label missing)** | **INARCO**
#E241
(1961)
6½″ Tall | **NAPCO**
(Paper Label)
#A5120
5½″ Tall |

| PLATE 28 | **NAPCOWARE**
#C6426
3½″ Tall | **NAPCOWARE**
#C6427
5″ Tall | **NAPCOWARE**
(Paper Label)
#C6428
6″ Tall | **NAPCOWARE**
#6429
7½″ Tall |

PLATE 29   JAPAN   NAPCO   NAPCO
         7″ Tall   #C1776   #C1775B
                5½″ Tall   7¼″ Tall

PLATE 30   ACME WARE   LEFTON'S   LEFTON'S
         6″ Tall   (Paper Label) (Paper Label)
                #2900   #4228
                6″ Tall   6″ Tall

PLATE 31	No Mark	NAPCO	NAPCO	NAPCO
	5″ Tall	#C1840	#C3282A	#C8589B
		(1956)	(1958)	(1956)
		6″ Tall	6″ Tall	6″ Tall

PLATE 32	No Mark	No Mark	No Mark	No Mark
	7″ Tall	6″ Tall	5¼″ Tall	6½″ Tall

(Could some of these be real people?)

PLATE 33	LEFTON	LEFTON	NAPCO	INARCO
	6″ Tall	6″ Tall	#C2636C	E1753
			6½″ Tall	6½″ Tall
			(1956)	

PLATE 34	ROBENS	NAPCOWARE	INARCO	JAPAN
	#501	#C5677	#E1062	5½″ Tall
	(1959)	5½″ Tall	(1963)	
	6½″ Tall		6″ Tall	

PLATE 35   **ROZART**   No Mark   No Mark   No Mark
                  (Paper Label)   4″ Tall   4¼″ Tall   5″ Tall
                  4½″ Tall

(I have been told these two are "Minnie Pearl.)

PLATE 36   **LEFTON'S**   **LEFTON'S**   **LEFTON'S**   **TILSO**
                  #1115   #1843   #1843   6″ Tall
                  5½″ Tall   5½″ Tall   5½″ Tall
                       (Same number, but different heads)

PLATE 37	NAPCO (Paper Label) #A5046 4½″ Tall	RUBENS #494 4½″ Tall	RUBENS #495 5¾″ Tall	NAPCO #C5046 4½″ Tall

PLATE 38	RUBENS #476 5″ Tall	RUBENS #477 6″ Tall	RUBENS #482 5″ Tall	RUBENS #4121 5½″ Tall

PLATE 39   **NAPCO**   **JAPAN**   **NAPCOWARE**   **NAPCOWARE**

NAPCO (Paper Label) #S93A 5″ Tall

JAPAN 5″ Tall

NAPCOWARE #C6431 6″ Tall

NAPCOWARE #C6430 5″ Tall

PLATE 40   **THAMES**   **No Mark**   **No Mark**   **PICO**

THAMES (Paper Label) 5½″ Tall

No Mark 4¼″ Tall

No Mark 5¼″ Tall

PICO (Paper Label) 6″ Tall

PLATE 41   No Mark   No Mark   Lrice   No Mark
                  4″ Tall   4″ Tall   (Paper Label)   4″ Tall
                                                    4″ Tall

PLATE 42   No Mark   No Mark   No Mark   No Mark
                  4½″ Tall   4″ Tall   4″ Tall   4½″ Tall

PLATE 43   **NAPCO**   **NAPCO**   **NAPCO**
         #C3307C   #C3815B   #C3815
         (1958)   (1959)   (1959)
         5½″ Tall   5½″ Tall   5½″ Tall
                (This one has brush eye
                   lashes)

PLATE 44   **No Mark**   **RELPO**   **No Mark**
         #E2188   #K936B   6″ Tall
         6″ Tall   6″ Tall

PLATE 45	INARCO #E480 (1961) 3½″ Tall	INARCO #E193/S (1961) 4½″ Tall	INARCO #E193/M (1961) 6″ Tall	INARCO #E779 (1962) 6¼″ Tall

PLATE 46	No Mark 5¼″ Tall	No Mark 6″ Tall	RUBENS #483 6½″ Tall	RUBENS #481 6½″ Tall

PLATE 47
This is a rather crude plaster head. It has a small juice glass embeded in the crown of the hat. 12″ Tall.

PLATE 48   No Mark
                  7¼″ Tall

PLATE 50

LEFTON'S	No Mark	NAPCO
#1086	#C5047	#C5675
6″ Tall	6½″ Tall	6″ Tall

PLATE 49   No Mark
                  8″ Tall

| PLATE 51 | No Mark
5½″ Tall | JAPAN
(Paper Label)
6″ Tall | INARCO
#E402
(1962)
5″ Tall | No Mark
6″ Tall |

| PLATE 52 | THAMES
(Paper Label)
5½″ Tall | ACME
4½″ Tall | LEFTON'S
#PY641
5″ Tall | MARGO
6″ Tall |

PLATE 53   No Mark   MADE IN   No Mark   No Mark

"Barbara"   JAPAN   6″ Tall   #2667

4¼″ Tall   6″ Tall   5″ Tall

(minor damage)

PLATE 54   No Mark   No Mark   JAPAN   JAPAN

4½″ Tall   5″ Tall   (Paper Label)   (Paper Label)

6″ Tall   5½″ Tall

(My daughter calls these "The Headache Ladies".)

PLATE 55   JAPAN   No Mark   JAPAN   JAPAN
                 6½″ Tall   6½″ Tall   4½″ Tall   6½″ Tall

PLATE 56   NAPCO   No Mark   No Mark
                 (Paper Label)   6½″ Tall   5½″ Tall
                 #S126B
                 5½″ Tall

PLATE 57   **No Mark**   **JAPAN**   **No Mark**
                    6¼″ Tall   (Paper Label)   7½″ Tall
                                        6″ Tall

PLATE 58   **No Mark**   **LEE WARDS**   **No Mark**
                    6″ Tall   (Paper Label)   5½″ Tall
                                        6½″ Tall

34

PLATE 59	No Mark 5¼″ Tall	NAPCO #3M2544 5½″ Tall	GLAMOUR GIRL 6½″ Tall	DESIGN #2 7″ Tall

PLATE 60	No Mark 6″ Tall	No Mark 6¼″ Tall	ROSE (1978) 7½″ Tall

PLATE 61   No Mark   No Mark   No Mark   U.S.A.
                  5″ Tall   4½″ Tall   6″ Tall   7″ Tall

PLATE 62 No Mark   No Mark   No Mark   INARCO   INARCO   No Mark
           3¼″ Tall   3¼″ Tall   2½″ Tall   #E1277   #E774   3¼″ Tall
                                    (1963)   (1963)

PLATE 63 No Mark   JAPAN   JAPAN   No Mark   No Mark   No Mark
           3½″ Tall   3″ Tall   3″ Tall   3″ Tall   3″ Tall   3½″ Tall

Young Ladies

PLATE 64   NAPCOWARE   NAPCOWARE   NAPCOWARE   NAPCOWARE
#C7313   #C7293   #C7294   #C7314
4½″ Tall   6″ Tall   7½″ tall   9″ Tall

PLATE 65   NAPCOWARE   NAPCOWARE   NAPCOWARE   NAPCOWARE
#C7471   #C7472   #C7473   #C7474
4½″ Tall   6″ Tall   7½″ Tall   9″ Tall

PLATE 66   **No Mark**   **RUBENS**   **BRINN'S**

7″ Tall   **#4157**   **(Paper Label)**

7″ Tall   **#2 TP-2444**

7½″ Tall

PLATE 67   **ROYAL CROWN**   **CAFFCO**   **RELPO**

#3411   **(Paper Label)**   **#1694-L**

7″ Tall   **#E3283**   **7½″ Tall**

7½″ Tall

PLATE 68	RELPO	INARCO	NAPCO
	#2055	#E3523	#C8500
	6″ Tall	7″ Tall	7″ Tall

PLATE 69	PARMA	LARK	RELPO
	(Paper Label)	(Paper Label)	#1783
	#A448	7″ Tall	7½″ Tall
	7″ Tall		

PLATE 70   No Mark   ENESCO   NAPCOWARE
                  #50/425   (Paper Label)   #C8501
                  8″ Tall   7″ Tall   8″ Tall

PLATE 71   BRINN'S   No Mark   No Mark
                  #TV-726   7″ Tall   7″ Tall
                  7″ Tall

PLATE 72   Handmade
                  Porcelain   The other three have a paper label ENESCO (fur col-
                  5¼″ Tall   lar original). 6″ Tall.

PLATE 73   ELJO   SAMPSON IMPORT   No Mark
                  (Paper Label)   #5543B   6½″ Tall
                  6″ Tall   (1964)   #3854
                                   6″ Tall

PLATE 74   RELPO   RELPO   RELPO
                  #K1175S   #K1175M   #K1175L
                  5″ Tall   5½″ Tall   6½″ Tall

PLATE 75   RUBENS   INARCO   VCAGCO   No Mark
              (Paper Label)   #E5623   (Paper Label)   5½″ Tall
              5½″ Tall   6½″ Tall   6″ Tall
              #484

PLATE 76   **TREMONT**   **No Mark**   **INARCO**
                (Paper Label)   7½″ Tall   #E6210
                6¼″ Tall   6½″ Tall

PLATE 77   **RELPO**   **RELPO**   **RELPO**
                #K1836   #K1679   #K1835
                7″ Tall   **7″ Tall**   **7½″ Tall**

PLATE 78　　　VELCO　　　　VELCO　　　　JAPAN　　　　VELCO
　　　　　　　#10759　　　#10758　　　5½″ Tall　　　#10761
　　　　　　　5½″ Tall　　　5½″ Tall　　　　　　　　　5½″ Tall

PLATE 79　　　RUBENS　　　RUBENS　　　No Mark　　　RUBENS
　　　　　　　#4105　　　　#4129　　　　6″ Tall　　　#4121
　　　　　　　6″ Tall　　　5½″ Tall　　　　　　　　　6″ Tall
(Be very careful when you wash these. The paint is not under glaze and comes off easily.)

PLATE 80

RELPO　　　　　　NAPCOWARE
#K1931　　　　　　#C7496
8½″ Tall　　　　　9½″ Tall

44

PLATE 81	No Mark 6″ Tall	NAPCO #3397 6″ Tall	No Mark 6″ Tall	Paper Label Nancy Pew 6″ Tall

PLATE 82	NAPCOWARE #C7494 6″ Tall	NAPCOWARE #C7495 7½″ Tall

PLATE 83   **NAPCO**   **NAPCO**   **No Mark**   **No Mark**

#C4899   **C5035C**   **5½″ Tall**   **5½″ Tall**

(1960)   **(1960)**

5½″ Tall   **5½″ Tall**

PLATE 84   **NAPCOWARE**   **CAFFCO**

(Paper Label)   **(Paper Label)**

#C8494   **#E-3142**

7″ Tall   **7″ Tall**

Plate 85   **No Mark**   **No Mark**   **No Mark**   **VCAGCO**

Plate 85

	No Mark	**No Mark**	**No Mark**	**VCAGCO**
	6½″ Tall	5½″ Tall	5½″ Tall	(Paper Label)
			(Wall Pocket)	5½″ Tall

PLATE 86	**No Mark**	**Paper Label**
	6½″ Tall	**NORCREST**
		#E-313

PLATE 87   No Mark   No Mark   No Mark
6½″ Tall   6″ Tall   6½″ Tall

(These are fine porcelain pieces)

PLATE 88   No Mark   JAPAN   No Mark
#1957   7½″ Tall   7½″ Tall
5½″ Tall

PLATE 89	HULL	CATALINA POTTER
	USA	#C 801
	#204	7″ Tall
	6″ Tall	

(Two very unusual pieces. I have only seen one other of the Catalina Pottery.)

PLATE 90	INARCO	INARCO	JAPAN	No Mark
	#E3548	#E3662	5½″ Tall	6″ Tall
	5½″ Tall	5½″ Tall		

| PLATE 91 | INARCO
#E2254
6″ Tall | RELPO
#K1696
5½″ Tall | INARCO
#E1610
(1964)
5″ Tall | No Mark
4½″ Tall |

| PLATE 92 | NAPCO
#C3205A
(1958)
6″ Tall | NAPCO
#C4072G
(1959)
6″ Tall | SHAFFORD
4½″ Tall |

PLATE 93   NAPCO   LEFTON'S   NAPCO
                  #C3812C   (Paper Label)   #C4414C
                  (1959)   #1343B   (1959)
                  6″ Tall   6″ Tall   6″ Tall

PLATE 94   NAPCOWARE   NAPCOWARE   NAPCOWARE
                  #CF6060   #C5938   #C5939
                  3½″ Tall   4½″ Tall   6″ Tall

PLATE 95   LEFTON'S   LEFTON'S   JAPAN   No Mark

(Paper Label)   (Paper Label)   6¼″ Tall   6″ Tall

#5920   #4596

5½″ TAll   6″ Tall

PLATE 96   ENESCO   INARCO   INARCO   PARMA

(Paper Label)   #E5622   #E2006   (Paper Label)

6″ Tall   5½″ Tall   6″ Tall   #A172

                                          5½″ Tall

| PLATE 97 | LARK
(Paper Label)
#JN-4112
5½″ Tall | ARDCO
(Paper Label)
#C3259
5½″ Tall | INARCO
#E5625
5½″ Tall | No Mark
5½″ Tall |

| PLATE 98 | UOAGCOCHINA
6″ Tall | No Mark
6¼″ Tall | No Mark
6½″ Tall |

PLATE 99   No Mark   RUBENS   No Mark
5¼″ Tall   (Paper Label)   6″ Tall
#493M
6″ Tall

PLATE 100   INARCO   ENESCO   No Mark
#E2104   (Paper Label)   7″ Tall
7″ Tall   6½″ Tall

PLATE 101   RUBENS   RUBENS   RUBENS   RUBENS
             #4183   #4123   #4104   #485
             6½″ Tall   6½″ Tall   6½″ Tall   6″ Tall
(These are very difficult to get in perfect condition because the paint is not baked on.)

PLATE 102   INARCO   INARCO   INARCO   RUBENS
             #E240   #E2005   #E1904   #4135
             (1961)   4½″ Tall   (1964)   5½″ Tall
             4½″ Tall   6½″ Tall

PLATE 103   **RELPO**   **RELPO**   **INARCO**   **No Mark**
                    #K1615   **#K1262**   **#E779**   5½″ Tall
                    5½″ Tall   5½″ Tall   (1962)
                                                         6″ Tall

PLATE 104   **VELCO**   **RELPO**   **VCAGCO**   **No Mark**
                    #3912C   **#K1406S**   5″ Tall   5″ Tall
                    5″ Tall   5½″ Tall

PLATE 105   **RELPO**   **JAPAN**   **No Mark**   **No Mark**
                 #K1053   **6″ Tall**   **5½″ Tall**   **6″ Tall**
                 6″ tall

PLATE 106   **RELPO**   **ENESCO**   **CAFFCO**   **NANCY PEW**
                 #K1694/S   **(Paper Label)** **(Paper Label)** **(Paper Label)**
                 5½″ Tall   **5½″ Tall**   **#E3145**   **#2262**
                                           5½″ Tall   **5½″ Tall**

PLATE 107   **LARK**   **No Mark**   **INARCO**   **RUBENS**
                (Paper Label)   5″ Tall   #E1062   #488
                5″ Tall   (1963)   6″ Tall
                                              6″ Tall

PLATE 108   **RELPO**   **BRINN'S**   **JAPAN**
                #1695   #T1821   No Number
                7″ Tall   7″Tall   7″ Tall
                              (Damaged)

PLATE 109   **RELPO**   **NAPCO**   **NAPCO**   **JAPAN**

                  #K937A   **#C3141B**   **#C3141A**   **No Number**

                  5½″ Tall   **(1958)**   **(1958)**   **6″ Tall**

                                 6½″ Tall   **6½″ Tall**

PLATE 110   **NAPCO**   **JAPAN**   **JAPAN**

                  #C3206B   **6″ Tall**   **6″ Tall**

                  (1958)

                  5½″ Tall

PLATE 111   **NAPCO**   **NANCY PEW**   **NAPCO**
          #C4553A   (Paper Label)   #C4556C
          (1960)   #2260   (1960)
          6" Tall   7" Tall   6¼" Tall

PLATE 112   **RELPO**   **INARCO**   **UNITED IMPORT**
          #K1761   #E3143   (Paper Label)
          7" Tall   7½" Tall   7" Tall

PLATE 113   No Mark   ENESCO   No Mark
                   7″ Tall   (Paper Label)   7½″ Tall
                                      7½″ Tall

PLATE 114   NANCY PEW   LEFTON'S   RELPO   CAFFCO
              (Paper Label)   (Paper Label)   #T961   (Paper Label)
                #7409   #6525   6″ Tall   #E3293
                6″ Tall   6″ Tall   6″ Tall

PLATE 115   **RUBENS**
(Paper Label)
#4135
5½″ Tall

RUBENS
(Paper Label)
#4137
7″ Tall

NAPCOWARE
(Paper Label)
#C8496
5½″ Tall

NAPCOWARE
(Paper Label)
#C8498
8″ Tall

PLATE 116   **INARCO**
#E3663
7½″ Tall

INARCO
#E4095
8″ Tall

NAPCOWARE
(Paper Label)
#C8497
7½″ Tall

PLATE 117   **UNITED IMPORT**   **ARDCO**   **INARCO**
(Paper Label)   (Paper Label)   #E5626
7″ Tall   7½″ Tall   7″ Tall

PLATE 118   **INARCO**   **ENESCO**   **CAFFCO**
#E6211   (Paper Label)   (Paper Label)
(Bisque)   7″ Tall   7″ Tall
5¼″ Tall

PLATE 119   **INARCO**   **No Mark**   **INARCO**
        #E1067   **7½″ Tall**   **#E2322**
        (1963)   **7½″ Tall**
        7″ Tall

PLATE 120   **VCAGCO**   **RELPO**   **JAPAN**   **RELPO**
        5½″ Tall   **#K1837**   **6″ Tall**   **#2012**
                  6″ Tall   **6″ Tall**

| PLATE 121 | INARCO
#E5624
5¼″ Tall | No Mark
6″ Tall | VCAGCO
(Paper Label)
5½″ Tall | RELPO
#2207
5½″ Tall |

| PLATE 122 | RELPO
#1661
5½″ Tall | RELPO
#K1947
5½″ Tall | INARCO
#E1063
(1963)
5½″ Tall | No Mark
6″ Tall |

| PLATE 123 | RICHARD
BENIT
#474
5″ Tall | RUBENS
(Paper Label)
#4107
6″ Tall | No Mark
5″ Tall | NANCY PEW
#7410
6½″ Tall |

| PLATE 124 | NAPCO
#C5708
(1962)
6″ Tall | NAPCO
#C5716
6″ Tall | NAPCO
#C5676
(1962) | LEFTON'S
#1227
6″ Tall |

PLATE 125 LEFTON'S   No Mark   SAMPSON IMPORT
      (Paper Label) 6″ Tall   #381A
      #70565   (1959)
      5½″ Tall   6¼″ Tall

PLATE 126 RELPO   ENESCO   INARCO   ENESCO
      #K1634   (Paper Label) #E1539   (Paper Label)
      6″ Tall   5½″ Tall   (1964)   5½″ Tall
                  6″ Tall

PLATE 127   **RELPO**   **INARCO**   **JAPAN**   **DABS**
                      #K1613   #E5882   5½″ Tall   (Paper Label)
                      5½″ Tall   6½″ Tall   D3221
                                                                  6¼″ Tall

PLATE 128   **JAPAN**   **NANCY PEW**   **RUBENS**   **RUBENS**
              (Paper Label)   (Paper Label)   #R488   (Paper Label)
               5½″ Tall   6″ Tall   6″ Tall   #R4130
                                                                6¼″ Tall

PLATE 129 **INARCO**   **NAPCO**   **ARDCO**   **PARMA**
       #E3394   **#C1615**   (Paper Label) (Paper Label)
       6″ Tall   **6″ Tall**   **6″ Tall**   **#A108**
                               6″ Tall

PLATE 130 **No Mark**   **HB**   **INARCO**   **NORLEANS**
       4½″ Tall   (Paper Label) **#E-1540** (Paper Label)
              4½″ Tall   **4½″ Tall**   **4½″ Tall**

PLATE 131	No Mark #4125 4½″ Tall	LEFTON'S (Paper Label) 4½″ Tall	NORLEANS (Paper Label) 4½″ Tall	No Mark 4½″ Tall	JAPAN #E3292 5″ Tall

PLATE 132	LEFTON #3130 4½″ Tall	NAPCO #C4897A (1960) 4½″ Tall	RELPO #K962 5″ Tall	RELPO #K860 6″ Tall

| PLATE 133 | No Mark
6″ Tall | KELVIA
#P 630
5½″ Tall | ENESCO
(Paper Label)
5½″ Tall | LEFTON'S
(Paper Label)
6″ Tall |

| PLATE 134 | NAPCO
#S 564
4″ Tall | NAPCO
#S 564
4″ Tall | NAPCO
#S 564
4″ Tall |

(Note everyone is different, but have same number)

| PLATE 135 | INARCO
#E 3403
6″ Tall | No Mark
5¼″ Tall | LEFTON'S
#6638
6½″ Tall | RUBENS
#498
5″ Tall |

PLATE 136   **22 KARAT**   No Mark   No Mark   **ORION**
                   GOLD   5″ Tall   5″ Tall   5″ Tall
                   U.S.A.
                   5½″ Tall

PLATE 137   **No Mark**   **No Mark**   **No Mark**
                   6½″ Tall   **5¼″ Tall**   **6″ Tall**

Teenagers

PLATE 138

INARCO
#E6106
7″ Tall

PLATE 139	**INARCO** **#E2967** **5½″ Tall**	**No Mark** **#4138** **6½″ Tall**	**RELPO** **#K1838** **5½″ Tall**	**NAPCOWARE** **#C8493** **5½″ Tall**

PLATE 140   NAPCOWARE   NAPCOWARE
                     #C8495   #C7314
                    8½″ Tall   8½″ Tall

PLATE 141   RELPO   LARK   No Mark
                    #2004   (Paper Label)   7½″ Tall
                   7″ Tall   #JN-4113
                                     7″ Tall

74

PLATE 142   Pair (left & right handed) Purchased separately. No mark. 6″ Tall.

| PLATE 143 | No Mark
5″ Tall | BRINN'S
#TP-2119
5½″ Tall | No Mark
ENESCO
(Paper Label)
5½″ Tall | No Mark
(JAPAN)
(Damaged)
6¼″ Tall |

| PLATE 144 | VCAGCO
(Paper Label)
5½″ Tall | No Mark
6″ Tall | JAPAN
5″ Tall |

PLATE 145   "HAPPY"   USA   VELCO   VELCO
(Bisque)   #408   (Paper Label)   #6691
4½" Tall   5" Tall   5" Tall   5½" Tall

PLATE 146   ENESCO   INARCO   No Mark   RUBENS
(Paper Label)   #3838   #4796   #4135
4½" Tall   5½" Tall   5¾" Tall   6" Tall

PLATE 147   INARCO   RELPO   INARCO   RELPO

	INARCO	RELPO	INARCO	RELPO
	#E6211	#2011	#E6211	#K2066
	5″ Tall	5½″ Tall	5″ Tall	5½″ Tall

(Note two different heads with same number)

	ROYAL CROWN	RELPO	RELPO	INARCO
PLATE 148	#3666	#K1942	#K1864	#E1064
	4½″ Tall	4½″ Tall	4½″ Tall	(1963)
				4½″ Tall

	JAPAN	NAPCOWARE	No Mark	RELPO
PLATE 149	5½″ Tall	(Paper Label)	6″ Tall	#2031
		#C3499		6″ Tall
		5½″ Tall		

PLATE 150   No Mark   JAPAN   PARMA   JAPAN
                   5½″ Tall   5½ Tall   #A-813   6″ Tall
                                                   5½″ Tall

PLATE 151   NANCY PEW   RUBENS   RELPO   RUBENS
                   (Paper Label)   #4136   #K-1614   #4103
                   6″ Tall   5½″ Tall   5″ Tall   6″ Tall

PLATE 152   JAPAN   BRIMM'S   SONSCO   No Mark
                        4½″ Tall   (Paper Label)   (Paper Label)   4¼″ Tall
                                 5″ Tall   4″ Tall

PLATE 153   ENESCO   No Mark   ENESCO   No Mark
                 (Paper Label) 4″ Tall   (Paper Label) 5″ Tall
                 4½″ Tall   4″ Tall

Famous People

PLATE 154

JACKIE KENNEDY ONASSIS

INARCO
#E1853
6½″ Tall
(Rare)

INARCO
#E1852
5½″ Tall

PLATE 155

ANNE BOLYEYN
ROYAL DOULTON
This was probably not meant to be for flowers, but it is a head non-the-less. 7″ Tall.

PLATE 156   **CHARLIE**   **BENJAMIN**

CHAPLAIN   **FRANKLIN**

5½″ Tall   6″ Tall

(Wall Pocket)

PLATE 157

SHIRLEY TEMPLE

6″ Tall

(I was told by the dealer that sold me this that
she was indeed Shirley, be your own judge!)

81

Oriental

PLATE 158   **JAPAN**   **JAPAN**   **UOAGCOCHINA**   No Mark
               5″ Tall   5¼″ Tall   5½″ Tall   4¾″ Tall

PLATE 159   **LRICE**   **No Mark**   **No Mark**
           (Paper Label)   8½″ Tall   4″ Tall
            5″ Tall

PLATE 160   No Mark   No Mark   No Mark
                      5″ Tall   6″ Tall   6½″ Tall

PLATE 161   (Paper Label)   No Mark   JAPAN
                     LEE WARDS   #3237   5″ Tall
                     5″ Tall   7½″ Tall

Religious

PLATE 162   **FLORET**   **RELPO**   **NAPCO**   **RELPO**
                          JAPAN   **(Paper Label)**   **(Paper Label)**   **#C1811**
                          6″ Tall   **6½″ Tall**   **5½″ Tall**   **5″ Tall**

PLATE 163   **No Mark**   **ROYAL SEALY**   **No Mark**
                          6″ Tall   **(Paper Label)**   **6″ Tall**
                                             6″ Tall

PLATE 164   **No Mark**   **NAPCOWARE**   **NAPCOWARE**
5½″ Tall   (Paper Label)   (Paper Label)
#R-7076   #R-7075
6½″ Tall   5″ Tall

PLATE 165   **ARDALT**   **No Mark**   **JAPAN**
(Paper Label)   8″ Tall   6″ Tall
6″ Tall

PLATE 166   HULL   Royal Wendsor   No Mark
                 #26   8″ Tall   6″ Tall
                 7″ Tall

PLATE 167   No Mark   No Mark   INARCO   No Mark
             5″ Tall   #4155   #E188/M   6½″ Tall
                            5½″ Tall   (1961)
                                           6″ Tall

Clowns

PLATE 168   **No Mark**   **No Mark**   **No Mark**   **No Mark**
                  #9115   4″ Tall   E92883   4″ Tall
                  6″ Tall   4½″ Tall

PLATE 169   **INARCO**   **NAPCOWARE**   **NAPCOWARE**   **INARCO**
                  #E-5071   #3321   #C3321   #E2320
                  4½″ Tall   6″ Tall   6″ Tall   5″ Tall

| PLATE 170 | NAPCOWARE
#1988
4¾″ Tall | No Mark
#7576
7″ Tall | RELPO
#6008
5½″ Tall | NAPCOWARE
#275
5½″ Tall |

| PLATE 171 | INARCO
No Number
7″ Tall | No Mark
#4498/A
7″ Tall | No Mark
5¼″ Tall |

| PLATE 172 | No Mark
(Wall Pocket)
6″ Tall | NAPCO
#IH-2243
6¼″ Tall | INARCO
#E-6730
5½″ Tall |

| PLATE 173 | No Mark
5¼″ Tall | No Mark
7″ Tall
(Paper Label)
National
Potteries | No Mark
5¼″ Tall
(Paper Label)
Inarco | No Mark
5½″ Tall |

Animals

PLATE 174

	HULL, USA	
#39	#37	#38
6″ Tall	(1955)	6″ Tall
	6″ Tall	

PLATE 175   Act WARE   LEFTON   No Mark
4″ Tall   (Paper Label)   5″ Tall
#H1953
6″ Tall

Art Deco

PLATE 176 No Mark 9¼" Tall

PLATE 177 MARTI HOLLYWOOD, 9½" Tall

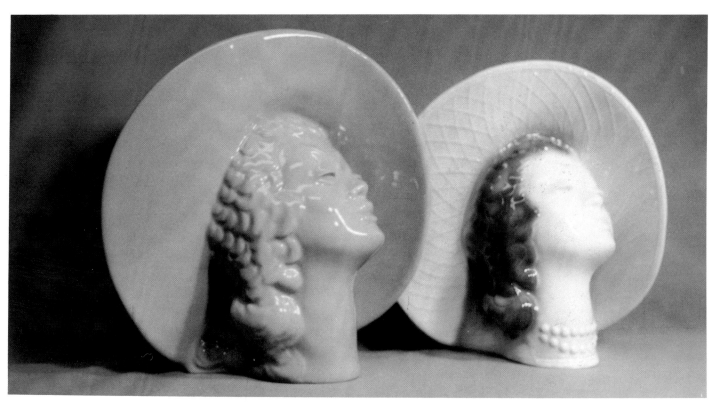

PLATE 178 No Mark
9" Tall

No Mark
7½" Tall

PLATE 179   No Mark   No Mark
                     8″ Tall   7″ Tall

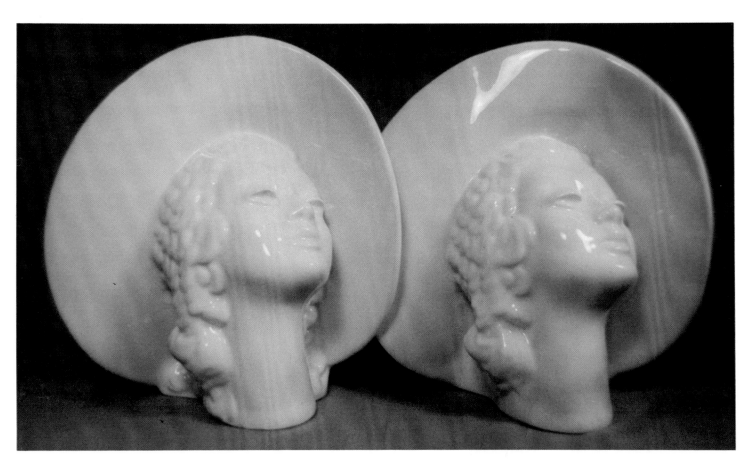

PLATE 180   USA   No Mark
                     8½″ Tall   Wall Pocket
                                        8½″ Tall
                                        (This one is
                                        scarce)

92

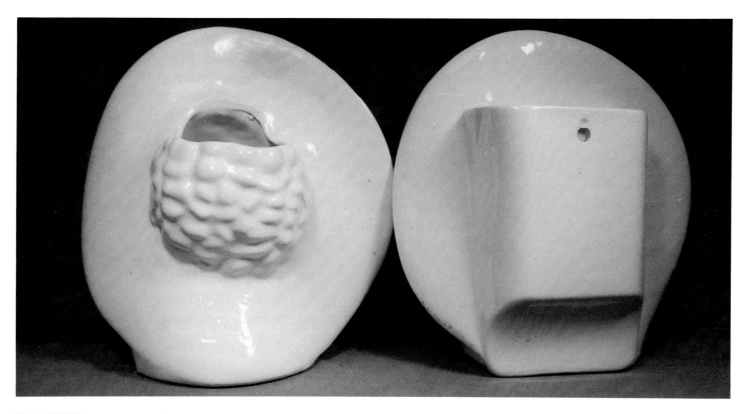

PLATE 181   Plate 180 pictured from the back so that you can see the difference in the two.

PLATE 182   U.S.A.   No Mark   JAPAN   U.S.A.
      4½″ Tall   5″ Tall   #KKS230A   #50N
      5½″ Tall   7½″ Tall

PLATE 183   **JAPAN**   **JAPAN**
7½″ Tall   7½″ Tall

PLATE 184   **No Mark**   **No Mark**   **BLOCK**   **No Mark**
5″ Tall   7″ Tall   6″ Tall   5½″ Tall
(Wall Pocket)   (Wall Pocket)

PLATE 185 No Mark   No Mark   JAPAN
     (MILK GLASS) 6¼" Tall 5½" Tall
     5¼" Tall

Men

PLATE 186 JAPAN   No Mark   LEFTON   No Mark
     4" Tall   3" Tall   (1956)   4½" Tall
                5½" Tall

PLATE 187   **ROYAL COPLEY**   **ROYAL COPLEY**
                                                (Wall Pocket)   (Original Paper Label
                                                7¾″ Tall   on hat brim)
                                                                 8½″ tall

PLATE 188   **UNCLE SAM**   **UNCLE SAM**   **OAKSHIRE**
                           No Mark   **MCCOY**   **VILLAGE**
                           6½″ Tall   **7½″ Tall**   **FLORIST**
                                                                       5½″ Tall

PLATE 189   CERAMICS (E. STAINBROOK)

These probably were not made for flowers, but are open heads.

Children

PLATE 190   VCAGCO
                       #8170B

This piece is rare, only one I have ever seen.

PLATE 191   No Mark   No Mark
                  8″ Tall   8″ Tall

These can sit or hang on the wall commonly called "Wall Pockets."

PLATE 192   THE DELSEY (TISSUE) GIRLS
Paper Label ENESCO
5″ Tall

PLATE 193	INARCO	INARCO	INARCO	INARCO
	6″ Tall	5″ Tall	5″ Tall	6″ Tall
	#E1579	#E778	#E978	E1579
	(1964)	(1962)	(1962)	(1964)
	CLEVE OHIO	CLEVE OHIO	CLEVE OHIO	CLEVE OHIO

PLATE 194   **GRADUATE**   **FIREMAN**   **SOLDIER**

#609   **INARCO**   **INARCO**

5¼″ Tall   **(Paper Label)**   **#E3250**

                            5″ Tall   **6″ Tall**

PLATE 195   **No Mark**   **No Mark**   **No Mark**

5″ Tall   **6″ Tall**   **5″ Tall**

PLATE 196   INARCO   INARCO   INARCO
                          #E3157   #E3157   #E2967
                          6″ Tall   6″ Tall   6½″ Tall

PLATE 197   RELIABLE   No Mark   RELIABLE
                       GLASSWARE   6″   GLASSWARE
                      #K679C (1956)   #K679B (1956)
                      6″ Tall   6″ Tall

| PLATE 198 | LEFTON'S
6″ Tall | INARCO
#2523
5½″ Tall | INARCO
#E2965
7″ Tall | No Mark
5½″ Tall |

| PLATE 199 | JAPAN
4½″ Tall | VCAGCO
(Paper Label)
6″ Tall | No Mark
6″ Tall | JAPAN
5½″ Tall |

PLATE 200   **LEFTON'S**   **LEFTON'S**   **PARMA**

(Paper Label)   **(Paper Label)**   **(Paper Label)**

6″ Tall   **6″ Tall**   **6″ Tall**

PLATE 201   **INARCO**   **INARCO**   **INARCO**

#E-2767   **#E2767**   **#E-2520**

5½″ Tall   **5½″ Tall**   **6½″ Tall**

PLATE 202   No Mark   (PY)   ENESCO
                   6¼″ Tall   5½″ Tall   (Paper Label)
                           (Flower petal   6½″ Tall
                           broken)

PLATE 203   No Mark   No Mark   GEO. Z. LEFTON
                   5¼″ Tall   5″ Tall   (1955)
                                         4½″ Tall

PLATE 204

NAPCO   No Mark   NAPCO
#IH1936   7″ Tall   #IH1936
6″ Tall   6″ Tall

PLATE 205   **RELPO**   **NAPCO**   **LIPPER & MANN**
                         #K1096   **#C1838C**   (Paper Label)
                       5½″ Tall   (1956)   6″ Tall
                                           6″ Tall

PLATE 206   **JAPAN**   **NAPCO**   **JOESEF**   **No Mark**
                 5½″ Tall   **#C4556B**   **ORIGINALS**   **#S207D**
                             (1960)   5″ Tall   6″ Tall
                             5″ Tall

PLATE 207 **RELPO**   **VCAGCO**   No Mark
       #K1097   (Paper Label)   6″ Tall
       5½″ Tall   8″ Tall

The head in the middle (above) is very unusual. The hat comes off. I have only seen one other.

PLATE 208 **INARCO**   **NAPCO**   **INARCO**   **INARCO**
      #E-1061   #C5037   #E1060   #E-1061
      4½″ Tall   5½″ Tall   5½″ Tall   (1963)
                          4½″ Tall

PLATE 209

ENESCO	INARCO	INARCO	NAPCOWARE
(Paper Label)	#E-3155	#E-3155	#C-7094
6″ Tall	5½″ Tall	5½″ Tall	4″ Tall

No Mark	No Mark	No Mark	No Mark
4¼″ Tall	#5B/378	6″ Tall	6″ Tall
	5″ Tall		
	(Damaged)		

PLATE 211

No Mark	No Mark	No Mark	JAPAN
5″ Tall	5¼″ Tall	5″ Tall	5″ Tall
	(Wall Pocket)		

PLATE 212   **ROYAL SEAL**   **INARCO**   **ORION**

(Paper Label)   **#E2183**   **(Paper Label)**

6″ Tall   **5½″ Tall**   **6½″ Tall**

PLATE 213   **JAPAN**   **NAPCO**   **INARCO**

5½″ Tall   **#C2634B**   **#E3157**

(1956)   **5½″ Tall**

5½″ Tall

PLATE 214   **No Mark**   **No Mark**   **GEO. Z. LEFTON**
                       5½″ Tall   **5½″ Tall**   **#50416**
                                                             (1956)
                                                          6″ Tall

PLATE 215   **MEXICO**   **No Mark**   **No Mark**   **No Mark**
                   5½″ Tall   **5″ Tall**   **4½″ Tall**   **5″ Tall**

PLATE 216   No Mark   RELPO   RELPO
5″ Tall   #2010   (Paper Label)
7″ Tall   5½″ Tall

PLATE 217   WALES   No Mark   No Mark
(Paper Label)   5½″ Tall   6″ Tall
6″ Tall

(These are bisque better quality heads)

| PLATE 218 | LEFTON
(Paper Label)
#2149
6½ Tall | No Mark
#4613
6½″ Tall | No Mark
5½″ Tall | LEFTON'S
#162
(1957)
5″ Tall |

| PLATE 219 | No Mark
4½″ Tall | VELCO
(Paper Label)
5½″ Tall
(Umbrella Girls) | JAPAN
5½″ Tall |

PLATE 220   Relpo   Relpo
                           #K1018B   #K1018A
                           8″ Tall   8″ Tall
These "Hummel" like heads are rare. This is the only pair I've ever seen. Both pieces have minor damage.

PLATE 221   No Mark   No Mark   Made In Japan   No Mark
               4¼″ Tall   4¼″ Tall   5″ Tall   S1725A
                                                                    5″ Tall

"Umbrella Girls"

111

PLATE 222   INARCO   INARCO   NAPCO   INARCO
#E1274   #E1274   #6541   #E1247
3½″ Tall   3¾″ Tall   3″ Tall   4″ Tall

PLATE 223   NAPCO   NAPCO   NAPCO
#CX2348B   #CX2707   #CX2708
5½″ Tall   6″ Tall   6½″ Tall
(1956)   (1957)   (1957)

PLATE 224   JAPAN   ENESCO   No Mark   JAPAN   OCCUPIED   OCCUPIED
3″ Tall   (Paper Label)   3″ Tall   3″ Tall   JAPAN   JAPAN
    3″ Tall   4¼″ Tall   4¼ Tall
(The first two are also place card holders)

PLATE 225	No Mark	No Mark	No Mark	No Mark	JAPAN	JAPAN
	3½″ Tall	2″ Tall	3½″ Tall	4″ Tall	3″ Tall	2½″ Tall

PLATE 226	No Mark	No Mark	RELPO	RELPO
	6″ Tall	6″ Tall	#6744	#6744
			5½″ Tall	5½″ Tall

PLATE 227	INARCO	No Mark	RELPO
	#E3156	#TP-2118	#2013
	5½″ Tall	6″ Tall	6″ Tall

PLATE 228   **RELPO**   **SAMSON IMPORT CO**
K1866   **#5359**
7″ Tall   (1966)
                                                      7½″ Tall

PLATE 229   **No Mark**   **E.O. BRODY**   **No Mark**
6¼″ Tall   **#A987**   5½″ Tall
                                     6½″ Tall

| PLATE 230 | No Mark
5½" Tall | Paper Label
ENESCO
5½" Tall | ENESCO
#2185
5" Tall |

| PLATE 231 | UOAGCOCHINA
5" Tall | ENESCO
#E-0491
5" Tall | ENESCO
#E-0491
5" Tall | RELPO
#459B
5" Tall |

PLATE 232   No Mark   No Mark   RUBENS   VIMAX
               5½″ Tall   6″ Tall   #602   (Paper Label)
                                         5¾″ Tall   5″ Tall

PLATE 233   No Mark   ENESCO   ENESCO
               6″ Tall   5″ Tall   5″ Tall

PLATE 234　　　　**INARCO**　　　　**SAMPSON**　　　　**RELPO**
(Paper Label)　　　#313A　　　　#6809
#E4392　　　　(1957)　　　　6″ Tall
6″ Tall　　　　5½″ Tall

PLATE 235　　　　**No Mark**　　　　**No Mark**　　　　**ENESCO**
5¼″ Tall　　　　4″ Tall　　　　(Paper Label)
5″ Tall

Wall Pockets

PLATE 236   ROYAL COPLEY   ROYAL COPLEY
8¼″ Tall   8″ Tall

PLATE 237   ROYAL COPLEY   ROYAL COPLEY
8½″ Tall   8½″ Tall

PLATE 238   ROYAL COPLEY   ROYAL COPLEY
                             7½″ Tall   7½″ Tall

PLATE 239   No Mark   No Mark   No Mark
                      7″ Tall   6¼″ Tall   5½″ Tall

PLATE 240   ROYAL COPLEY   ROYAL COPLEY
8″ Tall   8″ Tall

PLATE 241   No Mark   ROYAL COPLEY   ROYAL COPLEY   JAPAN
#214   6½″ Tall   6″ Tall   5″ Tall
6¾″ Tall   (damaged)

PLATE 242   JAPAN   NAPCO   JAPAN

PLATE 242

JAPAN
6½″ Tall

NAPCO
(Paper Label)
#S131 (5½″ Tall)
(Broken eye lash on right eye)

JAPAN
6½″ Tall

PLATE 243

JAPAN
(Man)
5½″ Tall

JAPAN
(Woman)
5¼″ Tall

NAPCO
(Paper Label)
#S238A
6″ Tall

LEFTON'S
(Paper Label)
"Ginger"
6¼″ Tall

PLATE 245   **JAPAN**   **JAPAN**   **No Mark**   **ENESCO**
                    4½″ Tall   4½″ Tall   5¼″ Tall   **(Paper Label)**
                                                                5½″ Tall

PLATE 244
This is a fine porcelain, probably French, by far the most valuable wall pocket in my collection. 11½″ Tall.

PLATE 246   **No Mark**   **RELPO**   **No Mark**   **ENESCO**
                 6½″ Tall   **(MARY LOU)**   6″ Tall   **(Paper Label)**
                               (1956)   6″ Tall
                               6″ Tall

PLATE 247   No Mark   GEO. Z.   No Mark   No Mark
                  6″ Tall   LEFTON   5¼″ Tall   6″ Tall
                                5″ Tall

PLATE 248   No Mark   No Mark   No Mark   VCAGCO
                  #S914   #S914   5¼″ Tall   5¼″ Tall
                  5¼″ Tall   5¼″ Tall

PLATE 249   **VCAGCO**   **VCAGCO**
              (Paper Label)   (Paper Label)
               4½″ Tall   4½″ Tall
         (An unusual ornamental wire hanger for these heads)

PLATE 250   **No Mark**   **VGAGCO**
               4½″ Tall   (Paper Label)

PLATE 251   "JEAN"   No Mark
          #231   7″ Tall
          7″ Tall

PLATE 252   No Mark   VCAGCO   No Mark
        #S688B   (Paper Label)   #S208A
        5″ Tall   6″ Tall   5½″ Tall

PLATE 253
No Mark
7½″ Tall

No Mark
8″ Tall

PLATE 254
No Mark
4½″ Tall

No Mark
4″ Tall

No Mark
4½″ Tall

No Mark
3½″ Tall

PLATE 255 **JAPAN** **JAPAN** **"JUNE"** No Mark
4½″ Tall 5″ Tall 4½″ Tall 5½″ Tall

PLATE 256 No Mark No Mark **NAPCO**
6″ Tall 8″ Tall (Paper Label)
#S154
5¾″ Tall

PLATE 257   No Mark   LEFTON'S   WALKER

                                        6" Tall   (Paper Label)   POTTERS

                                                     #S884   #901

                                                  7½" Tall   5½" Tall

PLATE 258   No Mark   No Mark   RELCO

                                8" Tall   5½" Tall   (Paper Label)

                                                                             #8A170

                                                                        6½" Tall

PLATE 259   No Mark   DO   NAPCOWARE
                             5″ Tall   6¼″ Tall   (Paper Label)
                                                     #6702

PLATE 260   LEFTON'S   No Mark   OCCUPIED
                             #542   7″ Tall   JAPAN
                            7½″ Tall   7″ Tall

Miscellaneous

PLATE 262 No Mark PRESTON CERAMICS
     7½″ Tall   7½″ Tall

PLATE 261
A modern terra cotta head ordered from gift catalog, 11½″ Tall.

PLATE 263 HAEGER No legible
    (Paper Label) mark, but head
    Wall Pocket is same as wall
    10″ Tall   pocket.

PLATE 264
Modern ceramics made especially for me. Heads are open with solid bottoms.
7½″ Tall & 9″ Tall.

| PLATE 265 | INARCO
#E-1611
(1964)
6″ Tall
(Damaged) | OCCUPIED
JAPAN
5½″ Tall | INARCO
#E-1611
(1964)
5½″ Tall |

| PLATE 266 | No Mark
#15/61
5½″ Tall | JAPAN
#100
4½″ Tall | NAPCO
4″ Tall | No Mark
5¼″ Tall |

PLATE 267   No Mark   No Mark   No Mark
3″ Tall   #3639   4″ Tall
7″ Tall
(I don't believe any of these were head vases, the first is probably a tooth pick holder and the other two are probably tobacco jars w/o lids.)

PLATE 268   JAPAN   UOAGCOCHINA   No Mark   No Mark   JAPAN
6½″ Tall   6½″ Tall   6″ Tall   6″ Tall   5″ Tall

PLATE 269   Iorice   Iorice   No Mark   No Mark

                  No Number   No Number   6½″ Tall   6½″ Tall

                  4″ Tall   4″ Tall   This is obviously a pair. Her head is
open, his is not. The bowl in his
hand is open.

PLATE 270   No Mark   No Mark   Relpo

                  5″ Tall   6″ Tall   #A149

                                                 6½″ Tall

These heads are not open, but each one has a vase in the back for flowers.

PLATE 271 JAPAN
4¼″ Tall
(Vase at
back)

JAPAN
4½″ Tall

No Mark
5½″ Tall

No Mark
6½″ Tall

No Mark
6½″ Tall

PLATE 272 No Mark
#50/423
4½″ Tall

RELPO
#6673
6½″ Tall

MODERN
CERAMIC
8½″ Tall

No Mark
7½″ Tall

(I consider these "rare," very few were made)

PLATE 273   "BECKY"   "BONNIE"   MEI-LENG

                                            5½" Tall   7" Tall   5" Tall

All the heads on this page were made by the "CERAMIC ARTS STUDIO," Madison, Wis., very fine pieces and quite expensive.

PLATE 274   "MANCHU"   "LOTUS"

                                            7½" Tall   8" Tall

PLATE 275   CONCHITA   RON CLARK'S   SHAWNEE
                   6″ Tall   POLY GIRL   #896
                                     6″ Tall   6″ Tall

PLATE 276   UOAGCOCHINA   CK   CALIFORNIA
                   (JAPAN)   7″ Tall   #52 W.H.H.
                   6″ Tall   6″ Tall

PLATE 277	NAPCOWARE #CX5409 4½″ Tall	"CHRISTMAS" INARCO #E195 (1961) 4½″ Tall	HOLT HOWARD (1959) 4″ Tall

PLATE 278	INARCO #E1138 (1963) 4″ Tall	No Mark 5″ Tall	WALT DISNEY PRODUCTIONS "SNOW WHITE" 5½″ Tall

PLATE 279   #1   #2   #3   #4   #23

These are modern called ''Sweet Keepers.'' I feel sure they were not made for flowers, but they are cute heads and this group is ''Christmas.'' I found these for $1.50 to $2.50 each. They are marked ''JASCO'' 1980 or 1981.

PLATE 280   #4   #7   #1   #3   #2

(Same as above)

138

Price Guide

All prices are left to right.

Plate 1.	$75.00	**Plate 61.**	$15.00; $12.50; $15.00; $20.00
Plate 2.	$32.50; $25.00; $20.00	**Plate 62.**	$15.00; $15.00; $15.00; $15.00; $15.00; $15.00
Plate 3.	$50.00	**Plate 63.**	$15.00; $15.00; $15.00; $15.00; $15.00; $15.00
Plate 4.	$30.00; $32.50; 32.50; $32.50	**Plate 64.**	$18.00; $22.50; $27.50; $50.00
Plate 5.	$85.00	**Plate 65.**	$18.00; $22.50; $27.50; $50.00
Plate 6.	$85.00	**Plate 66.**	$30.00; $30.00; $32.50
Plate 7.	$20.00; $20.00; $32.50	**Plate 67.**	$35.00; $35.00; $35.00
Plate 8.	$25.00; $25.00; $32.50; $32.50	**Plate 68.**	$25.00; $30.00; $30.00
Plate 9.	$20.00; $25.00; $30.00	**Plate 69.**	$35.00; $35.00; $35.00
Plate 10.	$20.00; $20.00; $20.00	**Plate 70.**	$50.00; $35.00; $40.00
Plate 11.	$25.00; $25.00; $20.00	**Plate 71.**	$35.00; $35.00; $37.50
Plate 12.	$20.00; $25.00; $25.00	**Plate 72.**	$15.00; $20.00; $25.00; $25.00
Plate 13.	$20.00; $20.00; $20.00; $25.00	**Plate 73.**	$25.00; $27.50; $25.00
Plate 14.	$25.00; $25.00; $25.00	**Plate 74.**	$25.00; $27.50; $32.50
Plate 15.	$20.00; $20.00; $25.00; $20.00	**Plate 75.**	$25.00; $27.50; $25.00; $22.50
Plate 16.	$20.00; $25.00; $25.00; $25.00	**Plate 76.**	$32.50; $37.50; $35.00
Plate 17.	$15.00; $25.00; $20.00; $30.00	**Plate 77.**	$35.00; $35.00; $37.50
Plate 18.	$25.00; $25.00; $25.00; $25.00	**Plate 78.**	$25.00; $25.00; $25.00; $25.00
Plate 19.	$20.00; $20.00; $25.00; $20.00	**Plate 79.**	$15.00; $15.00; $15.00; $17.50
Plate 20.	$35.00; $25.00; $32.50	**Plate 80.**	$40.00; $50.00
Plate 21.	$40.00; $35.00	**Plate 81.**	$17.50; $20.00; $20.00; $25.00
Plate 22.	$50.00; $45.00	**Plate 82.**	$27.50; $45.00
Plate 23.	$35.00; $40.00	**Plate 83.**	$20.00; $20.00; $20.00; $20.00
Plate 24.	$20.00; $25.00; $25.00; $25.00	**Plate 84.**	$30.00; $32.50
Plate 25.	$20.00; $20.00; $20.00; $25.00	**Plate 85.**	$25.00; $25.00; $30.00; $25.00
Plate 26.	$35.00; $25.00; $25.00; $32.50	**Plate 86.**	$30.00; $30.00
Plate 27.	$25.00; $25.00; $30.00; $25.00	**Plate 87.**	$35.00; $35.00; $35.00
Plate 28.	$15.00; $20.00; $25.00; $35.00	**Plate 88.**	$20.00; $32.50; $32.50
Plate 29.	$32.50; $25.00; $32.50	**Plate 89.**	$25.00; $45.00
Plate 30.	$25.00; $32.50; $32.50	**Plate 90.**	$20.00; $20.00; $20.00; $25.00
Plate 31.	$20.00; $30.00; $30.00; $30.00	**Plate 91.**	$20.00; $20.00; $25.00; $25.00
Plate 32.	$40.00; $35.00; $35.00; $40.00	**Plate 92.**	$25.00; $25.00; $20.00
Plate 33.	$25.00; $25.00; $35.00; $35.00	**Plate 93.**	$25.00; $25.00; $25.00
Plate 34.	$35.00; $25.00; $30.00; $25.00	**Plate 94.**	$20.00; $25.00; $27.50
Plate 35.	$20.00; $15.00; $20.00; $20.00	**Plate 95.**	$20.00; $25.00; $25.00; $25.00
Plate 36.	$20.00; $20.00; $20.00; $15.00	**Plate 96.**	$25.00; $17.50; $25.00; $20.00
Plate 37.	$20.00; $20.00; $25.00; $20.00	**Plate 97.**	$20.00; $20.00; $20.00; $20.00
Plate 38.	$15.00; $20.00; $15.00; $15.00	**Plate 98.**	$35.00; $35.00; $35.00
Plate 39.	$25.00; $25.00; $25.00; $20.00	**Plate 99.**	$15.00; $25.00; $25.00
Plate 40.	$20.00; $15.00; $20.00; $25.00	**Plate 100.**	$30.00; $30.00; $35.00
Plate 41.	$20.00; $20.00; $20.00; $20.00	**Plate 101.**	$15.00; $15.00; $15.00; $15.00
Plate 42.	$20.00; $20.00; $20.00; $20.00	**Plate 102.**	$20.00; $20.00; $25.00; $20.00
Plate 43.	$25.00; $25.00; $25.00	**Plate 103.**	$20.00; $20.00; $20.00; $20.00
Plate 44.	$25.00; $25.00; $25.00	**Plate 104.**	$20.00; $25.00; $20.00; $25.00
Plate 45.	$18.00; $20.00; $30.00; $30.00	**Plate 105.**	$25.00; $25.00; $25.00; $25.00
Plate 46.	$25.00; $27.50; $25.00; $25.00	**Plate 106.**	$25.00; $20.00; $20.00; $25.00
Plate 47.	$20.00	**Plate 107.**	$20.00; $20.00; $25.00; $25.00
Plate 48.	$40.00-$45.00	**Plate 108.**	$32.50; $10.00; $32.50
Plate 49.	$40.00-$45.00	**Plate 109.**	$25.00; $30.00; $30.00; $30.00
Plate 50.	$25.00; $25.00; $25.00	**Plate 110.**	$25.00; $25.00; $25.00
Plate 51.	$25.00; $25.00; $20.00; $25.00	**Plate 111.**	$25.00; $30.00; $25.00
Plate 52.	$25.00; $15.00; $15.00; $25.00	**Plate 112.**	$35.00; $35.00; $35.00
Plate 53.	$20.00; $25.00; $25.00; $10.00	**Plate 113.**	$35.00; $37.50; $37.50
Plate 54.	$15.00; $15.00; $20.00; $20.00	**Plate 114.**	$20.00; $20.00; $20.00; $20.00
Plate 55.	$25.00; $25.00; $20.00; $25.00	**Plate 115.**	$25.00; $35.00; $25.00; $45.00
Plate 56.	$25.00; $28.50; $25.00	**Plate 116.**	$35.00; $45.00; $40.00
Plate 57.	$25.00; $25.00; $32.50	**Plate 117.**	$35.00; $35.00; $35.00
Plate 58.	$25.00; $25.00; $15.00	**Plate 118.**	$25.00; $32.50; $32.50
Plate 59.	$12.50; $15.00; $17.50; $17.50	**Plate 119.**	$30.00; $32.50; $35.00
Plate 60.	$15.00; $20.00; $25.00	**Plate 120.**	$25.00; $25.00; $25.00; $25.00
		Plate 121.	$25.00; $25.00; $25.00; $25.00

Plate 122.	$25.00; $25.00; $25.00; $27.50
Plate 123.	$20.00; $20.00; $20.00; $27.50
Plate 124.	$24.00; $25.00; $25.00; $25.00
Plate 125.	$25.00; $25.00; $30.00
Plate 126.	$25.00; $20.00; $25.00; $22.50
Plate 127.	$20.00; $30.00; $20.00; $30.00
Plate 128.	$25.00; $20.00; $20.00; $27.50
Plate 129.	$20.00; $20.00; $20.00; $25.00
Plate 130.	$15.00; $15.00; $15.00; $15.00
Plate 131.	$15.00; $15.00; $15.00; $15.00; $15.00
Plate 132.	$16.00; $16.50; $20.00; $25.00
Plate 133.	$25.00; $25.00; $25.00; $25.00
Plate 134.	$15.00; $15.00; $15.00
Plate 135.	$20.00; $25.00; $25.00; $20.00
Plate 136.	$25.00; $20.00; $25.00; $25.00
Plate 137.	$15.00; $20.00; $25.00
Plate 138.	$32.50
Plate 139.	$25.00; $30.00; $20.00; $20.00
Plate 140.	$45.00; $45.00
Plate 141.	$32.50; $32.50; $35.00
Plate 142.	$35.00; $35.00
Plate 143.	$20.00; $25.00; $25.00; $10.00
Plate 144.	$25.00; $25.00; $25.00
Plate 145.	$15.00; $20.00; $25.00; $25.00
Plate 146.	$15.00; $25.00; $25.00; $25.00
Plate 147.	$25.00; $25.00; $25.00; $25.00
Plate 148.	$15.00; $15.00; $15.00; $15.00
Plate 149.	$25.00; $25.00; $25.00; $25.00
Plate 150.	$25.00; $20.00; $25.00; $20.00
Plate 151.	$20.00; $20.00; $25.00; $20.00
Plate 152.	$20.00; $20.00; $20.00; $25.00
Plate 153.	$20.00; $15.00; $20.00; $20.00
Plate 154.	$140.00; $120.00
Plate 155.	$125.00
Plate 156.	$40.00; $45.00-$55.00
Plate 157.	$25.00
Plate 158.	$20.00; $25.00; $25.00; $20.00
Plate 159.	$20.00; $45.00; $15.00
Plate 160.	$20.00; $25.00; $25.00
Plate 161.	$25.00; $35.00; $25.00
Plate 162.	$20.00; $35.00; $25.00; $25.00
Plate 163.	$25.00; $25.00; $27.50
Plate 164.	$15.00; $25.00; $20.00
Plate 165.	$25.00; $35.00; $25.00
Plate 166.	$30.00; $35.00; $25.00
Plate 167.	$15.00; $20.00; $25.00; $15.00
Plate 168.	$15.00; $15.00; $15.00; $15.00
Plate 169.	$15.00; $20.00; $20.00; $15.00
Plate 170.	$15.00; $20.00; $15.00; $15.00
Plate 171.	$20.00; $20.00; $15.00
Plate 172.	$25.00; $25.00; $15.00
Plate 173.	$15.00; $15.00; $15.00; $15.00
Plate 174.	$30.00; $30.00; $30.00
Plate 175.	$12.50; $15.00; $15.00
Plate 176.	$75.00
Plate 177.	$135.00
Plate 178.	$45.00; $45.00
Plate 179.	$40.00; $40.00
Plate 180.	$35.00; $55.00
Plate 181.	See plate 180
Plate 182.	$15.00; $20.00; $15.00; $25.00
Plate 183.	$30.00; $30.00
Plate 184.	$15.00; $25.00; $20.00; $20.00
Plate 185.	$10.00; $25.00; $15.00
Plate 186.	$15.00; $15.00; $25.00; $15.00
Plate 187.	$35.00; $35.00
Plate 188.	$25.00; $35.00; $15.00
Plate 189.	$20.00 each
Plate 190.	$65.00
Plate 191.	$30.00 pair
Plate 192.	$35.00 each
Plate 193.	$20.00; $20.00; $20.00; $25.00
Plate 194.	$25.00; $25.00; $25.00
Plate 195.	$20.00; $30.00; $20.00
Plate 196.	$25.00; $25.00; $25.00
Plate 197.	$25.00; $25.00; $25.00
Plate 198.	$25.00; $25.00; $30.00; $25.00
Plate 199.	$15.00; $25.00; $25.00; $25.00
Plate 200.	$25.00; $25.00; $25.00
Plate 201.	$20.00; $20.00; $25.00
Plate 202.	$20.00; $5.00; $25.00
Plate 203.	$20.00; $20.00; $20.00
Plate 204.	$20.00; $25.00; $25.00
Plate 205.	$25.00; $25.00; $25.00
Plate 206.	$25.00; $20.00; $20.00; $25.00
Plate 207.	$25.00; $45.00; $35.00
Plate 208.	$15.00; $20.00; $20.00; $15.00
Plate 209.	$20.00; $20.00; $20.00; $15.00
Plate 210.	$15.00; $7.00; $20.00; $20.00
Plate 211.	$20.00; $20.00; $20.00; $20.00
Plate 212.	$25.00; $20.00; $25.00
Plate 213.	$25.00; $25.00; $20.00
Plate 214.	$20.00; $15.00; $8.00
Plate 215.	$15.00; $15.00; $15.00; $15.00
Plate 216.	$20.00; $35.00; $25.00
Plate 217.	$30.00; $30.00; $30.00
Plate 218.	$25.00; $25.00; $25.00; $25.00
Plate 219.	$25.00; $25.00; $25.00
Plate 220.	$25.00 pair
Plate 221.	$25.00; $25.00; $25.00; $25.00
Plate 222.	$15.00; $15.00; $15.00; $15.00
Plate 223.	$25.00; $25.00; $30.00
Plate 224.	$15.00; $15.00; $15.00; $15.00; $30.00 pair
Plate 225.	$15.00; $15.00; $15.00; $15.00; $10.00; $10.00
Plate 226.	$20.00; $20.00; $20.00; $20.00
Plate 227.	$25.00; $25.00; $20.00
Plate 228.	$25.00; $25.00
Plate 229.	$20.00; $25.00; $20.00
Plate 230.	$20.00; $20.00; $20.00
Plate 231.	$20.00; $20.00; $20.00; $20.00
Plate 232.	$20.00; $20.00; $20.00; $20.00
Plate 233.	$25.00; $20.00; $20.00
Plate 234.	$20.00; $20.00; $20.00
Plate 235.	$20.00; $15.00; $20.00
Plate 236.	$35.00; $35.00
Plate 237.	$30.00; $30.00
Plate 238.	$20.00; $20.00
Plate 239.	$20.00; $20.00; $20.00
Plate 240.	$30.00; $30.00
Plate 241.	$25.00; $20.00; $5.00; $15.00
Plate 242.	$25.00; $7.00; $25.00
Plate 243.	$35.00; $35.00; $35.00; $35.00
Plate 244.	$100.00
Plate 245.	$20.00; $20.00; $20.00; $20.00
Plate 246.	$20.00; $20.00; $25.00; $25.00
Plate 247.	$20.00; $20.00; $20.00; $20.00

Plate 248. $25.00; $25.00; $20.00; $20.00
Plate 249. $20.00; $20.00
Plate 250. $20.00; $20.00
Plate 251. $25.00; $25.00
Plate 252. $20.00; $25.00; $20.00
Plate 253. $25.00; $25.00
Plate 254. $15.00; $15.00; $15.00; $15.00
Plate 255. $20.00; $20.00; $20.00; $20.00
Plate 256. $15.00; $25.00; $20.00
Plate 257. $15.00; $25.00; $15.00
Plate 258. $25.00; $15.00; $25.00
Plate 259. $15.00; $20.00; $15.00
Plate 260. $65.00; $65.00; $75.00
Plate 261. $25.00
Plate 262. $15.00; $10.00
Plate 263. $10.00; $20.00
Plate 264. $15.00; $20.00

Plate 265. $5.00; $25.00; $25.00
Plate 266. $20.00; $15.00; $12.50; $15.00
Plate 267. $25.00; $50.00; $25.00
Plate 268. $25.00; $25.00; $20.00; $20.00; $25.00
Plate 269. $10.00; $10.00; $25.00; $25.00
Plate 270. $25.00; $25.00; $25.00
Plate 271. $20.00; $25.00; $20.00; $25.00; $25.00
Plate 272. $30.00; $50.00; $25.00; $35.00
Plate 273. $50.00; $65.00; $50.00
Plate 274. $75.00; $75.00
Plate 275. $15.00; $25.00; $25.00
Plate 276. $25.00; $20.00; $20.00
Plate 277. $15.00; $20.00; $15.00
Plate 278. $20.00; $25.00; $35.00
Plate 279. $4.00; $4.00; $4.00; $4.00; $4.00
Plate 280. $4.00; $4.00; $4.00; $4.00; $4.00

Books on Antiques and Collectibles

Most of the following books are available from your local book seller or antique dealer, or on loan from your public library. If you are unable to locate certain titles in your area you may order by mail from COLLECTOR BOOKS, P.O. Box 3009, Paducah, KY 42002-3009. Add $2.00 for postage for the first book ordered and $.25 for each additional book. Include item number, title and price when ordering. Allow 14 to 21 days for delivery. All books are well illustrated and contain current values.

Books on Glass and Pottery

1810	American Art Glass, Shuman	$29.95
1517	American Belleek, Gaston	$19.95
2016	Bedroom & Bathroom Glassware of the Depression Years	$19.95
1312	Blue & White Stoneware, McNerney	$9.95
1959	Blue Willow, 2nd Ed., Gaston	$14.95
1627	Children's Glass Dishes, China & Furniture II, Lechler	$19.95
1892	Collecting Royal Haeger, Garmon	$19.95
1373	Collector's Ency of American Dinnerware, Cunningham	$24.95
2133	Collector's Ency. of Cookie Jars, Roerig	$24.95
2017	Collector's Ency. of Depression Glass, Florence, 9th Ed.	$19.95
1812	Collector's Ency. of Fiesta, Huxford	$19.95
1439	Collector's Ency. of Flow Blue China, Gaston	$19.95
1961	Collector's Ency. of Fry Glass, Fry Glass Society	$24.95
2086	Collector's Ency. of Gaudy Dutch & Welsh, Schuman	$14.95
1813	Collector's Ency. of Geisha Girl Porcelain, Litts	$19.95
1915	Collector's Ency. of Hall China, 2nd Ed., Whitmyer	$19.95
1358	Collector's Ency. of McCoy Pottery, Huxford	$19.95
1039	Collector's Ency. of Nippon Porcelain I, Van Patten	$19.95
1350	Collector's Ency. of Nippon Porcelain II, Van Patten	$19.95
1665	Collector's Ency. of Nippon Porcelain III, Van Patten	$24.95
1447	Collector's Ency. of Noritake, Van Patten	$19.95
1037	Collector's Ency. of Occupied Japan I, Florence	$14.95
1038	Collector's Ency. of Occupied Japan II, Florence	$14.95
1719	Collector's Ency. of Occupied Japan III, Florence	$14.95
2019	Collector's Ency. of Occupied Japan IV, Florence	$14.95
1715	Collector's Ency. of R.S. Prussia II, Gaston	$24.95
1034	Collector's Ency. of Roseville Pottery, Huxford	$19.95
1035	Collector's Ency. of Roseville Pottery, 2nd Ed., Huxford	$19.95
1623	Coll. Guide to Country Stoneware & Pottery, Raycraft	$9.95
2077	Coll. Guide Country Stone. & Pottery, 2nd Ed., Raycraft	$14.95
1523	Colors in Cambridge, National Cambridge Society	$19.95
1425	Cookie Jars, Westfall	$9.95
1843	Covered Animal Dishes, Grist	$14.95
1844	Elegant Glassware of the Depression Era, 4th Ed., Florence	$19.95
2024	Kitchen Glassware of the Depression Years, 4th Ed., Florence	$19.95
1465	Haviland Collectibles & Art Objects, Gaston	$19.95
1917	Head Vases Id & Value Guide, Cole	$14.95
1392	Majolica Pottery, Katz-Marks	$9.95
1669	Majolica Pottery, 2nd Series, Katz-Marks	$9.95
1919	Pocket Guide to Depression Glass, 7th Ed., Florence	$9.95
1438	Oil Lamps II, Thuro	$19.95
1670	Red Wing Collectibles, DePasquale	$9.95
1440	Red Wing Stoneware, DePasquale	$9.95
1958	So. Potteries Blue Ridge Dinnerware, 3rd Ed., Newbound	$14.95
1889	Standard Carnival Glass, 2nd Ed., Edwards	$24.95
1814	Wave Crest, Glass of C.F. Monroe, Cohen	$29.95
1848	Very Rare Glassware of the Depression Years, Florence	$24.95
2140	Very Rare Glassware of the Depression Years, Second Series	$24.95

Books on Dolls & Toys

1887	American Rag Dolls, Patino	$14.95
2079	Barbie Fashion, Vol. 1, 1959-1967, Eames	$24.95
1749	Black Dolls, Gibbs	$14.95
1514	Character Toys & Collectibles 1st Series, Longest	$19.95
1750	Character Toys & Collectibles, 2nd Series, Longest	$19.95
2021	Collectible Male Action Figures, Manos	$14.95
1529	Collector's Ency. of Barbie Dolls, DeWein	$19.95
1066	Collector's Ency. of Half Dolls, Marion	$29.95
2151	Collector's Guide to Tootsietoys, Richter	$14.95
2082	Collector's Guide to Magazine Paper Dolls, Young	$14.95
1891	French Dolls in Color, 3rd Series, Smith	$14.95
1631	German Dolls, Smith	$9.95
1635	Horsman Dolls, Gibbs	$19.95
1067	Madame Alexander Collector's Dolls, Smith	$19.95
2025	Madame Alexander Price Guide #15, Smith	$7.95
1995	Modern Collector's Dolls, Vol. I, Smith	$19.95
1516	Modern Collector's Dolls Vol. V, Smith	$19.95
1540	Modern Toys, 1930-1980, Baker	$19.95

2033	Patricia Smith Doll Values, Antique to Modern, 6th Ed.	$9.95
1886	Stern's Guide to Disney	$14.95
2139	Stern's Guide to Disney, 2nd Series	$14.95
1513	Teddy Bears & Steiff Animals, Mandel	$9.95
1817	Teddy Bears & Steiff Animals, 2nd, Mandel	$19.95
2084	Teddy Bears, Annalees & Steiff Animals, 3rd, Mandel	$19.95
2028	Toys, Antique & Collectible, Longest	$14.95
1648	World of Alexander-Kins, Smith	$19.95
1808	Wonder of Barbie, Manos	$9.95
1430	World of Barbie Dolls, Manos	$9.95

Other Collectibles

1457	American Oak Furniture, McNerney	$9.95
1846	Antique & Collectible Marbles, Grist, 2nd Ed.	$9.95
1712	Antique & Collectible Thimbles, Mathis	$19.95
1880	Antique Iron, McNerney	$9.95
1748	Antique Purses, Holiner	$19.95
1868	Antique Tools, Our American Heritage, McNerney	$9.95
2015	Archaic Indian Points & Knives, Edler	$14.95
1426	Arrowheads & Projectile Points, Hothem	$7.95
1278	Art Nouveau & Art Deco Jewelry, Baker	$9.95
1714	Black Collectibles, Gibbs	$19.95
1666	Book of Country, Raycraft	$19.95
1960	Book of Country Vol II, Raycraft	$19.95
1811	Book of Moxie, Potter	$29.95
1128	Bottle Pricing Guide, 3rd Ed., Cleveland	$7.95
1751	Christmas Collectibles, Whitmyer	$19.95
1752	Christmas Ornaments, Johnston	$19.95
1713	Collecting Barber Bottles, Holiner	$24.95
2132	Collector's Ency. of American Furniture, Vol. I, Swedberg	$24.95
2018	Collector's Ency. of Graniteware, Greguire	$24.95
2083	Collector's Ency. of Russel Wright Designs, Kerr	$19.95
1634	Coll. Ency. of Salt & Pepper Shakers, Davern	$19.95
2020	Collector's Ency. of Salt & Pepper Shakers II, Davern	$19.95
2134	Collector's Guide to Antique Radios, Bunis	$16.95
1916	Collector's Guide to Art Deco, Gaston	$14.95
1753	Collector's Guide to Baseball Memorabilia, Raycraft	$14.95
1537	Collector's Guide to Country Baskets, Raycraft	$9.95
1437	Collector's Guide to Country Furniture, Raycraft	$9.95
1842	Collector's Guide to Country Furniture II, Raycraft	$14.95
1962	Collector's Guide to Decoys, Huxford	$14.95
1441	Collector's Guide to Post Cards, Wood	$9.95
1716	Fifty Years of Fashion Jewelry, Baker	$19.95
2022	Flea Market Trader, 6th Ed., Huxford	$9.95
1668	Flint Blades & Proj. Points of the No. Am. Indian, Tully	$24.95
1755	Furniture of the Depression Era, Swedberg	$19.95
2081	Guide to Collecting Cookbooks, Allen	$14.95
1424	Hatpins & Hatpin Holders, Baker	$9.95
1964	Indian Axes & Related Stone Artifacts, Hothem	$14.95
2023	Keen Kutter Collectibles, 2nd Ed., Heuring	$14.95
1181	100 Years of Collectible Jewelry, Baker	$9.95
2137	Modern Guns, Identification & Value Guide, Quertermous	$12.95
1965	Pine Furniture, Our Am. Heritage, McNerney	$14.95
2080	Price Guide to Cookbooks & Recipe Leaflets, Dickinson	$9.95
1124	Primitives, Our American Heritage, McNerney	$8.95
1759	Primitives, Our American Heritage, 2nd Series, McNerney	$14.95
2026	Railroad Collectibles, 4th Ed., Baker	$14.95
1632	Salt & Pepper Shakers, Guarnaccia	$9.95
1888	Salt & Pepper Shakers II, Guarnaccia	$14.95
2141	Schroeder's Antiques Price Guide, 9th Ed.	$12.95
2096	Silverplated Flatware, 4th Ed., Hagan	$14.95
2027	Standard Baseball Card Pr. Gd., Florence	$9.95
1922	Standard Bottle Pr. Gd., Sellari	$14.95
1966	Standard Fine Art Value Guide, Huxford	$29.95
2085	Standard Fine Art Value Guide Vol. 2, Huxford	$29.95
2078	The Old Book Value Guide, 2nd Ed	$19.95
1923	Wanted to Buy	$9.95
1885	Victorian Furniture, McNerney	$9.95

Schroeder's Antiques Price Guide

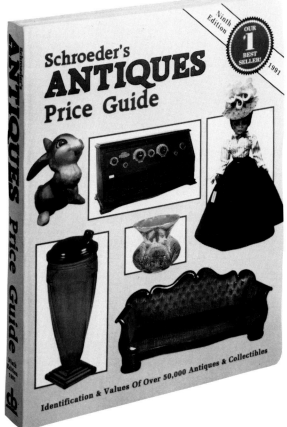

Schroeder's Antiques Price Guide has become THE household name in the antiques & collectibles field. Our team of editors work year-round with more than 200 contributors to bring you our #1 best-selling book on antiques & collectibles.

With more than 50,000 items identified & priced, Schroeder's is a must for the collector & dealer alike. If it merits the interest of today's collector, you'll find it in Schroeder's. Each subject is represented with histories and background information. In addition, hundreds of sharp original photos are used each year to illustrate not only the rare and unusual, but the everyday "fun-type" collectibles as well -- not postage stamp pictures, but large close-up shots that show important details clearly.

Our editors compile a new book each year. Never do we merely change prices. Accuracy is our primary aim. Prices are gathered over the entire year previous to publication, from ads and personal contacts. Then each category is thoroughly checked to spot inconsistencies, listings that may not be entirely reflective of actual market dealings, and lines too vague to be of merit. Only the best of the lot remains for publication. You'll find Schroeder's Antiques Price Guide the one to buy for factual information and quality.

No dealer, collector or investor can afford not to own this book. It is available from your favorite bookseller or antiques dealer at the low price of $12.95. If you are unable to find this price guide in your area, it's available from Collector Books, P.O. Box 3009, Paducah, KY 42002-3009 at $12.95 plus $2.00 for postage and handling.

8½ x 11", 608 Pages   **$12.95**

COLLECTOR BOOKS

A Division of Schroeder Publishing Co., Inc.